Remarkable Writers

Lois Lowry

Lily Erlic

www.av2books.com

RAP 843 2504

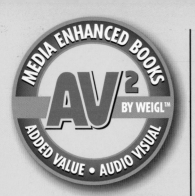

AV² provides enriched content that supplements and complements this book. Weigl's AV² books strive to create inspired learning and engage young minds in a total learning experience.

Your AV² Media Enhanced books come alive with...

Audio
Listen to sections of the book read aloud.

Key Words
Study vocabulary, and complete a matching word activity.

Video
Watch informative video clips.

Quizzes
Test your knowledge.

Embedded Weblinks
Gain additional information for research.

Slide Show
View images and captions, and prepare a presentation.

Try This!
Complete activities and hands-on experiments.

... and much, much more!

Go to **www.av2books.com**, and enter this book's unique code.

BOOK CODE

R268176

AV² by Weigl brings you media enhanced books that support active learning.

Published by AV² by Weigl
350 5th Avenue, 59th Floor
New York, NY 10118

Website: www.weigl.com www.av2books.com

Library of Congress Control Number: 2013953145

ISBN 978-1-4896-0664-8 (hardcover)
ISBN 978-1-4896-0665-5 (softcover)
ISBN 978-1-4896-0666-2 (single-user eBook)
ISBN 978-1-4896-0667-9 (multi-user eBook)

Printed in the United States of America, in North Mankato, Minnesota
1 2 3 4 5 6 7 8 9 0 18 17 16 15 14

012014
WEP301113

Senior Editor: Heather Kissock
Design: Terry Paulhus

Weigl acknowledges Getty Images, Alamy, Lois Lowry, and the University of Southern Maine as its primary photo suppliers for this title.

Remarkable Writers

Contents

AV² Book Code 2

Introducing Lois Lowry 4

Early Life... 6

Growing Up... 8

Developing Skills... 10

Timeline of Lois Lowry...................................... 12

Early Achievements 14

Tricks of the Trade 16

Remarkable Books 18

From Big Ideas to Books 22

Lois Lowry Today 24

Fan Information 26

Write a Biography 28

Test Yourself... 29

Writing Terms 30

Key Words/Index 31

Log on to www.av2books.com 32

Introducing Lois Lowry

Millions of people read Lois Lowry's books. **Settings** in her books are descriptive, vivid, and clear. Some characters in Lois's books are based on herself or people that she has known.

Her first book, *A Summer to Die*, is loosely based on the life of Lois's sister. In the story, sisters Meg and Molly do not get along. Eventually, they begin to become friends. Then Molly learns that she has a disease called leukemia. She soon dies. *A Summer to Die* is a sad story.

〰 Lois is very approachable to her readers. She has been known to sign books that fans mail to her.

Writers are often inspired to record the stories of people who lead interesting lives. The story of another person's life is called a biography. A biography can tell the story of any person, from authors such as Lois Lowry, to inventors, presidents, and sports stars.

When writing a biography, authors must first collect information about their subject. This information may come from a book about the person's life, a news article about one of his or her accomplishments, or a review of his or her work. Libraries and the internet will have much of this information. Most biographers will also interview their subjects. Personal accounts provide a great deal of information and a unique point of view. When some basic details about the person's life have been collected, it is time to begin writing a biography.

As you read about Lois Lowry, you will be introduced to the important parts of a biography. Use these tips and the examples provided to learn how to write about an author or any other remarkable person.

Lois's memories of her life experiences have been woven into fiction. She take events that happened in her own life and shapes them into stories.

Number the Stars, another book by Lois Lowry, won an award called the Newbery Medal. The book tells of a friendship between two girls and how they help a family escape from the Germans during World War II. *The Giver*, another Newbery Medal winner, is a novel about a boy living in a **futuristic** society.

The **themes** in Lois's books are about human relationships. Her characters show friendship, courage, love, and hope. Lois writes from her heart.

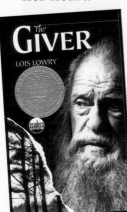
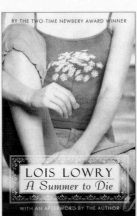

Early Life

Lois Lowry has traveled to and lived in many places. She was born on Oahu, Hawai'i, on March 20, 1937. Her family had a house in the town of Waianae. Lois was the middle child. She had an older sister, Helen, and a younger brother, Jon. Lois's father, Robert Hammersberg, was an army dentist. Her mother, Katherine Landis, was a homemaker.

"Nothing 'inspired' me to be an author. It was simply what I always wanted to do, from childhood, what I did best, loved best. If anything inspired me, it was books."
— *Lois Lowry*

Lois learned to read when she was 3 years old. Her mother and father encouraged her to read. Her mother read books to Lois. Lois's father told stories of his youth. In 1941, Pearl Harbor, Hawai'i, was bombed. Lois's father had to leave the family. He served on a hospital ship during World War II. He eventually went to Japan. Lois spent these years with her brother, sister, mother, and grandparents in her mother's hometown, Carlisle, Pennsylvania. Her grandfather often read her poems. She spent many of her childhood days at the public library. Lois knew that she would become a writer one day.

When Lois was born, Waianae was a small town. Today, the city attracts many tourists.

At school, Lois was very advanced in reading and writing. She skipped grade 2. At first, Lois enjoyed grade 3. One day, she received a multiplication assignment. Lois did not even know how to add and subtract. Multiplication terrified her. Lois suffered from what she called "math anxiety" throughout school. Still, her love of reading was much greater than her fear of math.

Lois was a shy, quiet child. She would rather spend time with a good book than playing with friends. Lois's reading was like training for when she became a writer. She learned about language and how stories develop. Lois's **vocabulary** increased. She could put words on paper and create wonderful stories.

A person's early years have a strong influence on his or her future. Parents, teachers, and friends can have a large impact on how a person thinks, feels, and behaves. These effects are strong enough to last throughout childhood, and often a person's lifetime.

In order to write about a person's early life, biographers must find answers to the following questions.

1 Where and when was the person born?

2 What is known about the person's family and friends?

3 Did the person grow up in unusual circumstances?

✍ Helen is 3 years older than Lois. Their brother, Jon, was born when Lois was 6 years old.

Growing Up

Lois's father remained in Japan after World War II ended. In 1948, Lois and her family moved to Japan to be reunited with him. Lois and her family lived with other American families in a community called Washington Heights. They lived in different types of houses, ate different types of food, and wore different clothes than the Japanese. The community had its own church, movie theater, library, and elementary school.

> "In blue jeans and sneakers..., I explore my way comfortably around the huge, sprawling, noisy, crowded city (Tokyo) by bike and bus and train without a qualm."
> —Lois Lowry

Sometimes, Lois snuck out of the community. She rode her bicycle down the street to observe Japanese life. Lois ate Japanese foods with her friends. Lois and her sister attended Meguro School in Japan. They learned many new things about Japanese **culture**.

Get to Know Japan

N

RUSSIA

CHINA

Sea of Japan

NORTH KOREA

SOUTH KOREA

Yellow Sea

Washington Heights

JAPAN

★ Tokyo

Pacific Ocean

East China Sea

LEGEND

☐ Japan ☐ Land ☐ Water
Borders ● City ★ Capital City

SCALE 0
500 Kilometers   500 Miles

Lois loved Japan. The years she lived there influenced her writing. Although Lois has never written about her experiences living in Tokyo, she remembers it helped her learn about cultural differences. The Japanese way of life was different from her own. Lois learned about the geography of Japan, as well. Lois would never have developed a sense of how other cultures live if she had stayed in a small town in the United States.

Often Lois explored the area called Shibuya in Tokyo. She describes what she saw, "It is crowded with shops and people and theaters and street vendors and the day-to-day bustle of Japanese life." Lois remembers the smells of charcoal and fish fertilizers, and the sounds of music, wooden sticks, and wooden **geta**. Lois recalls the schoolchildren dressed in dark blue uniforms.

Writing About
Growing Up

Some people know what they want to achieve in life from a very young age. Others do not decide until much later. In any case, it is important for biographers to discuss when and how their subjects make these decisions. Using the information they collect, biographers try to answer the following questions about their subjects' paths in life.

1 Who had the most influence on the person?

2 Did he or she receive assistance from others?

3 Did the person have a positive attitude?

On special occasions, Lois sometimes dressed in traditional Japanese clothing, including a kimono.

Developing Skills

In 1951, Lois and her family moved to Governors Island in New York City. Lois's father gave her a typewriter for her thirteenth birthday. She appreciated this generous gift. She used the typewriter in high school and college.

Lois learned that her sister, Helen, was dying of cancer. Years later, Lois wrote about the emotional experience in her first novel, *A Summer to Die.*

In high school, Lois won a national award for student writing. She then attended Pembroke College, the women's branch of Brown University, located in Rhode Island. Lois enjoyed college. Her English professor told her she wrote well, but lacked life experience. Lois thought otherwise. She felt that she had many experiences to share.

📖 Lois and her family lived at Fort Jay on Governors Island. The fort is now a national historic site.

After 2 years of college, Lois left school. She married a naval officer named Donald Grey Lowry in 1956. The couple moved to San Diego, California, where Donald was stationed. Together, they had four children. Alix was born in Connecticut in 1958. Grey was born in Florida in 1959. Kristin was born in 1961, and Benjamin was born in 1962. Both children were born in Massachusetts.

While living in Cambridge, Massachusetts, Lois learned that her sister, Helen, was dying of cancer. Sadly, Helen died in 1962 before Lois could visit her. Years later, Lois wrote about the emotional experience in her first novel, *A Summer to Die*.

Lois was only 19 years old when she married Donald in 1956.

Writing About Developing Skills

Every remarkable person has skills and traits that make him or her noteworthy. Some people have natural talent, while others practice diligently. For most, it is a combination of the two. One of the most important things that a biographer can do is to tell the story of how the subject developed his or her talents.

1 What was the person's education?

2 What was the person's first job or work experience?

3 What obstacles did the person overcome?

Timeline of Lois Lowry

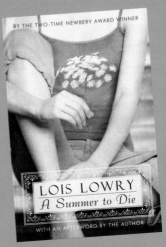

1977

Lois's first book, *A Summer to Die*, is published.

1937

Lois is born on March 20, in the Hawai'ian capital city, Honolulu.

1972

Lois graduates from the University of Southern Maine with a Bachelor of Arts degree.

1948

Lois lives in Japan and learns about Japanese culture.

1956

Lois marries Donald Lowry, a naval officer.

1990

Lois wins the Newbery Medal for her novel, *Number the Stars*.

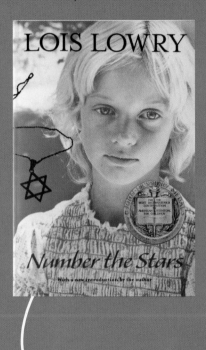

2012

Son, the final book in the *The Giver* quartet, is released in October.

1994

Lois wins another Newbery Medal, this time for *The Giver*.

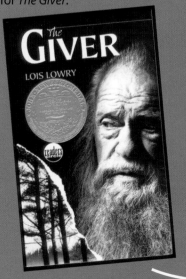

2007

The American Library Association awards Lois the Margaret Edwards Award for her contribution to writing for young adults.

2004

Lois is awarded the Christopher Medal for her book *The Silent Boy*. This award is presented to people who have produced books and movies with high moral standards.

Early Achievements

When Lois was an adult and her children were attending school, she decided to return to school herself. Lois attended the University of Southern Maine. She received a bachelor of arts degree in 1972, the same year that Alix graduated from high school. Lois went to **graduate school**, studying photography and literature.

"I love the process of putting words on a page, rearranging them, making them work somehow, hearing them slip into a sequence that sounds right . . ." —*Lois Lowry*

Lois fulfilled a childhood dream when she began writing in the 1970s. At first, she wrote stories for newspapers and magazines. Lois wrote simple stories that reflected her own life. Then, a children's book **editor** asked if Lois would like to write for children. Lois said she would. Instead of completing graduate school, Lois decided to finish writing her first book. When she was 59 years old, the University of Southern Maine gave Lois an **honorary degree**.

The University of Southern Maine was founded in 1878. Today, more than 7,000 students attend classes there.

In 1976, Lois finished writing *A Summer to Die*. The novel was published the following year. The book is somewhat **autobiographical**. The story is about the death of a young girl and how it affects her family. Many of Lois's books are about making connections with others.

Lois creates characters before she begins writing a story. She imagines her characters as real people. In Lois's imagination, they have names and faces. She can also hear them speaking. When Lois has a good sense of who her characters are and how they act, she sets a series of events in motion. This is how she writes her stories.

Lois's marriage ended in 1977, the same year her first book was published. Two years later, she moved from Maine to Boston, Massachusetts. In 1980, she met a man named Martin, with whom she shared her life. Together, they have six grown children and nine grandchildren.

Writing About
Early Achievements

No two people take the same path to success. Some people work very hard for a long time before achieving their goals. Others may take advantage of a fortunate turn of events. Biographers must make special note of the traits and qualities that allow their subjects to succeed.

1 What was the person's most important early success?

2 What processes does the person use in his or her work?

3 Which of the person's traits was most helpful in his or her work?

Lois and Martin traveled the world together, visiting exotic locales such as Europe, Africa, and Antarctica.

Tricks of the Trade

Lois Lowry worked hard to become a good writer. She studied writing at university, where she **honed** her writing skills. Here are some tips that may help you improve your writing.

Reading

Most writers read a great deal. They visit libraries and bookstores. Exploring books helps writers improve their writing. Ask your teacher, librarian, or bookseller for suggestions about which books to read. Read a wide range of authors, and eventually you will develop your own style of writing.

Take Writing Courses

There are many writing courses available for children and young adults. A community or recreation center may offer courses on journaling or creative writing. Lois took many courses in writing through college and university. Taking a course will help you practice so that you can learn to write well.

Lois recommends writing letters to a friend or grandparent to practice writing. The letters should be written as though telling a story.

Find Your Own Space

Most writers have a special place where they write. Lois Lowry writes in an office in her home. Find your own space where you can write. Perhaps it is a corner of a room or a desk. Keep your notepads, pens, or computer at your special writing spot. Having your own area is important. It will help you concentrate on your writing.

"Reading is the most productive thing for me, I think. If I read brilliant paragraphs I want to rush out and write brilliant paragraphs." —*Lois Lowry*

Rewrite

After a writer completes a first **draft** of the story, he or she makes changes. Rewriting makes the story better. Some writers finish the first draft, put it away, and then read it again a few days later. This allows the writer to think about the story. Lois Lowry rewrites until she is happy with her words. Then Lois sends the story to her publisher. Most times the publisher will ask Lois to make more changes.

📖 Lois sometimes feels embarrassed to show people her office. She feels it is disorganized.

Remarkable Books

Lois Lowry enjoys writing for children. She has written for adults, but Lois is best known for her novels for children and young adults. She writes historical fiction, science fiction, and fantasy.

Number the Stars

In *Number the Stars*, Lois writes a story of friendship and courage. She tells of a close friendship between two girls and a caring family who help others. Ten-year-old Annemarie Johansen lives in Denmark in 1943, during World War II. The Germans **occupy** Denmark. Annemarie's best friend is Ellen Rosen. Ellen is Jewish. She must hide in Annemarie's house, away from the German soldiers. The soldiers are trying to evacuate all the Jewish people from Denmark. Annemarie's family wants to help their friends the Rosens. Soon, the family realizes that Ellen is no longer safe with them. Annemarie helps her friend and others escape to the safety of Sweden.

AWARDS
Number the stars
1989 School Library Journal, Best Books of the Year
1990 Newbery Medal

The Giver

The Giver is one of Lois Lowry's most popular books. Many middle school and high school children in classrooms all over the world read this book. In *The Giver*, Lois creates a society with different rules. In this futuristic story, the main character is a boy named Jonas. In his community, no one can make choices. The Committee of Elders makes decisions for everyone. The rest of the community follows the rules set out for them. Jonas's society has no disease or crime. The people have no memories. One day, the Committee of Elders decides to make Jonas the receiver of memories. Jonas receives all the memories of history, war, pain, snow, and colors. Along with the memories, he also receives wisdom to make choices. He chooses to leave the community. Jonas sets out to create a new future because he realizes his community is not as perfect as he thought it was. Jonas experiences many new things outside the community.

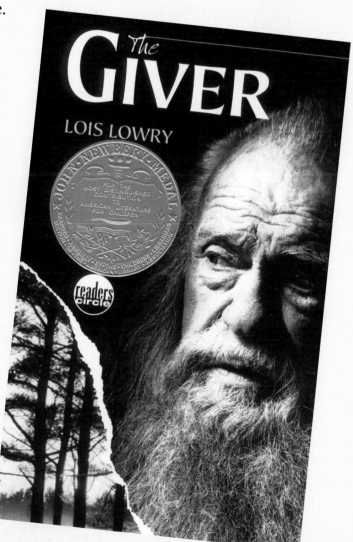

Anastasia Krupnik

Anastasia Krupnik is a funny story. It is the first book in a series of books about Anastasia Krupnik. Anastasia is a 10-year-old girl. She writes her thoughts and makes a list in her green notebook. On her list, she writes everything she hates and everything she likes. Her parents tell her that they are going to have a baby. She places "parents" and "babies" on her hate list. *Anastasia Krupnik* will make readers laugh out loud.

Anastasia, Absolutely

In *Anastasia, Absolutely*, Anastasia is in grade 8. Anastasia has a dog, which she walks every morning before school. One morning, she makes a big mistake. Anastasia's mother asks her to mail some drawings to her publisher. Instead of putting her mother's drawings in the mailbox, she drops the bag she used to pick up after her dog into the mailbox. Read this book to learn how Anastasia tries to correct her mistake.

All About Sam

Sam is Anastasia Krupnik's lovable younger brother. He has appeared as a character in many Anastasia books. This story covers Sam's life from the time he is a newborn until he is a toddler. Sam takes readers on many adventures. He has his own ideas about haircuts, nursery school, and eating broccoli.

By the Two-Time Newbery Award Winner
Lois Lowry

GOONEY BIRD GREENE

Gooney Bird Greene

Gooney Bird Greene, a second grader, arrives at Waterford Elementary School wearing pajamas and cowboy boots. Her classmates decide that they want to hear Gooney Bird Greene's story at story time. The teacher allows Gooney Bird to tell stories to the class. The stories are creative and exaggerated. Gooney Bird enjoys being the center of attention. Every day, she tells a **far-fetched** story. One story is called, "How Gooney Bird Came from China on a Flying Carpet." The story is actually true. Gooney Bird came from a town called China. She was rolled up inside a carpet, which flew out of the car. Gooney Bird's classmates enjoyed listening to her tales. You will, too!

AWARDS
Gooney Bird Greene
2002 Parents' Choice Silver Award
2002 New York Public Library-100 Titles for Reading and Sharing

From Big Ideas to Books

Before writing her first novel, Lois wrote stories for magazines. She wrote stories about children for adults. Lois wrote about herself and her family. She wrote about life after World War II.

Lois's novel, *Number the Stars*, won the Newbery Medal in 1990. The award is very respected. Winning the award helped Lois become successful. *Number the Stars* is based on a true story. Lois's friend, Annelise Platt, was a child in Denmark during World War II. Annelise told Lois about the horrors of war. Annelise described cold homes during winter. She talked about how her sister died during childbirth because no professional medical care was available. Lois wrote Annelise's story for children.

Winning the Newbery Medal helped Lois become successful.

Lois **submitted** her work to a publisher called Bantam Doubleday Dell Books for Young Readers. They published the book. Many people asked Lois to speak at schools about *Number the Stars*. Children all over the world read the book, which was translated into twenty languages.

The Publishing Process

Publishing companies receive hundreds of **manuscripts** from authors each year. Only a few manuscripts become books. Publishers must be sure that a manuscript will sell many copies. As a result, publishers reject most of the manuscripts they receive. Once a manuscript has been accepted, it goes through

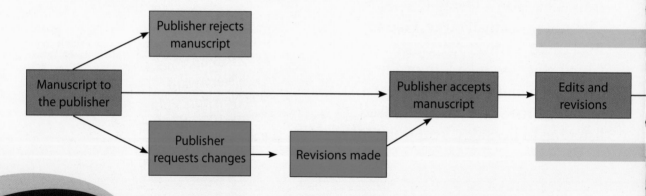

The Giver also won the Newbery Medal. Although the book was well written, some parents objected to it. These parents did not want their children to read about a **totalitarian** society. Lois is pleased that the book creates discussions in classrooms all over the world. Lois has since written three more books, *Gathering Blue, Messenger,* and *Son,* that have some of the same characters as *The Giver.* These three books are considered a quartet.

📖 Although *Number the Stars* is a work of fiction, its events are based around the real-life occupation of Denmark by Nazi Germany during World War II.

many stages before it is published. Often, authors change their work to follow an editor's suggestions. Once the book is published, some authors receive royalties. This is money based on book sales.

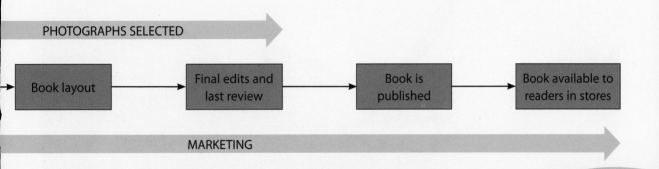

PHOTOGRAPHS SELECTED

Book layout → Final edits and last review → Book is published → Book available to readers in stores

MARKETING

Lois Lowry Today

Lois Lowry continues to publish books regularly. She has now written and published more than 40 books. In 2007, the American Library Association honored Lois's contribution to teenage fiction with the Margaret Edwards Award. Lois has a regular writing schedule. She writes for nearly five hours each weekday. She listens to classical music and drinks coffee while she writes.

Writing has helped Lois through difficult times. Whenever something painful or unhappy happened in her life, she wrote. Lois's son, Grey, became a fighter pilot. He died in 1995. Lois misses him terribly. Grey's death was a sad time for Lois, but her family and her writing gave her comfort.

✍ Lois had two sons, Ben and Grey. Lois named many of her characters after Ben.

Sadly, in 2011, Lois's partner of thirty years, Martin, died. Lois continues to live in an old farmhouse the couple shared in Maine. She lives there with Alfie, a Tibetan terrier, and a cat named Lulu. She is visited often by her grandchildren.

Lois divides her time between the farmhouse and another home in Cambridge, Massachusetts. In this house, Lois has original paintings on the wall, given to her by **illustrator** friends. Bookshelves full of books fill most rooms in the house.

Lois has given speeches at many conventions and conferences. Teachers and librarians attend to hear Lois speak. She talks about her books and their meaning. Her books continue to inspire other writers. When *The Giver* was released, its tale of a futuristic totalitarian society was considered ground-breaking. The book used its setting to raise issues and problems that are facing people today. Many current children's and young adult novels use similar settings and devices.

Writing About the Person Today

The biography of any living person is an ongoing story. People have new ideas, start new projects, and deal with challenges. For their work to be meaningful, biographers must include up-to-date information about their subjects. Through research, biographers try to answer the following questions.

1 Has the person received awards or recognition for accomplishments?

2 What is the person's life's work?

3 How have the person's accomplishments served others?

Lois's house in Maine was built in 1768.

Fan Information

If you want to know more about Lois Lowry, you should read a book that Lois wrote called *Looking Back*. The book is full of pictures and memories from Lois's life. *Looking Back* tells how many of Lois's life experiences became stories. In the book, Lois also answers many questions her fans have asked.

Many of Lois's books have been translated into different languages. Her books are popular in classrooms all over the United States, as well. Lois's books have **stimulated** students' minds and promoted discussions across the country.

✎ Fans can learn more about Lois's life and works online at her website. Lois regularly writes blog posts about her life and travels, and invites readers to email her with questions or comments.

After Lois wrote *The Giver*, many fans wrote her emails and letters asking about the ending. They wanted to know more about what happened to the main character, Jonas. Lois wrote three more companion books to satisfy her curious readers. The last book, *Son*, was published in 2012. *The Giver* continues to be a fan favorite. A film adaptation of the popular novel is set to be released in 2014.

Lois has an interesting website for fans who want to learn more about her life and her work. On her site, Lois answers frequently asked questions. She also regularly updates fans on her blog.

A film version of *The Giver* is planned for release in 2014. It stars Brenton Thwaites and Taylor Swift.

Write a Biography

All of the parts of a biography work together to tell the story of a person's life. Find out how these elements combine by writing a biography. Begin by choosing a person whose story fascinates you. You will have to research the person's life by using library books and reliable websites. You can also e-mail the person or write him or her a letter. The person might agree to answer your questions directly.

Use a concept web, such as the one below, to guide you in writing the biography. Answer each of the questions listed using the information you have gathered. Each heading on the concept web will form an important part of the person's story.

Parts of a Biography

Early Life

Where and when was the person born?

What is known about the person's family and friends?

Did the person grow up in unusual circumstances?

Growing Up

Who had the most influence on the person?

Did he or she receive assistance from others?

Did the person have a positive attitude?

Developing Skills

What was the person's education?

What was the person's first job or work experience?

What obstacles did the person overcome?

Person Today

Has the person received awards or recognition for accomplishments?

What is the person's life's work?

How have the person's accomplishments served others?

Early Achievements

What was the person's most important early success?

What processes does the person use in his or her work?

Which of the person's traits were most helpful in his or her work?

Test Yourself

1 Where was Lois Lowry born?

2 Does Lois have any brothers or sisters?

3 What country did Lois live in when she was 11 to 13 years of age?

4 What college did Lois attend after high school?

5 What university did Lois attend when she was 36 years of age?

6 What was the name of Lois's first novel?

7 How many children did Lois have?

8 What is Lois's advice to writers about writing?

9 What is the name of the first book in Lois's quartet?

10 Where does Lois live now?

ANSWERS

1. Lois Lowry was born in Oahu, Hawai'i. 2. Yes, Lois has a younger brother named Jon. Her older sister, Helen, died of cancer. 3. Japan 4. Lois attended Pembroke college, the women's branch of Brown University. 5. University of Southern Maine 6. A Summer to Die 7. four 8. Lois Lowry's advice is for writers to read many books. 9. The Giver 10. Lois lives in Cambridge, Massachusetts and Maine.

Writing Terms

The field of writing has its own language. Understanding some of the more common writing terms will allow you to discuss your ideas about books.

action: the moving events of a work of fiction

antagonist: the person in the story who opposes the main character

autobiography: a history of a person's life written by that person

biography: a written account of another person's life

character: a person in a story, poem, or play

climax: the most exciting moment or turning point in a story

episode: a scene or short piece of action in a story

fiction: stories about characters and events that are not real

foreshadow: hinting at something that is going to happen later in the book

imagery: a written description of a thing or idea that brings an image to mind

narrator: the speaker of the story who relates the events

nonfiction: writing that deals with real people and events

novel: published writing of considerable length that portrays characters within a story

plot: the order of events in a work of fiction

protagonist: the leading character of a story; often a likable character

resolution: the end of the story, when the conflict is settled

scene: a single episode in a story

setting: the place and time in which a work of fiction occurs

theme: an idea that runs throughout a work of fiction

Key Words

autobiographical: based on the author's own life

culture: the customs, traditions, and names of a nation or people

draft: a rough copy of something written

editor: a person who makes changes in a book

far-fetched: hard to believe

futuristic: something that takes place after the present

geta: a Japanese wooden-soled shoe

graduate school: a school that grants master's degrees and/or doctorates, degrees that are more advanced than a bachelor's degree

honed: perfected a skill

honorary degree: a degree given as an award or honor; the recipient does not have to complete the usual requirements

illustrator: an artist who creates pictures for books, magazines, etc.

manuscripts: drafts of stories sent to a publisher

occupy: to take control of a place, especially during war

settings: places and times in which works of fiction occur

stimulated: excited

submitted: to send to a publisher for possible publication

themes: ideas that run throughout works of fiction

totalitarian: a system of government in which the ruler controls the social, political, economic, intellectual, cultural, and religious activities

vocabulary: words of a language

Index

All About Sam 21
Anastasia, Absolutely 20
Anastasia Krupnik 20

Brown University 10, 29

Cambridge, Massachusetts 11, 25, 29

Gathering Blue 23
Giver, The 5, 13, 19, 23, 25, 27, 29
Gooney Bird Greene 21

Japan 6, 8, 9, 12, 29

Looking Back 26

Meguro School 8
Messenger 23

New York City 10
Number the Stars 5, 13, 18, 22, 23

Oahu, Hawai'i 6, 29

Shibuya 9
Son 13, 23, 27
Summer to Die, A 4, 10, 11, 12, 15, 29

Tokyo 8, 9

University of Southern Maine 12, 14, 29

Washington Heights 8
World War II 6, 8, 18, 22, 23

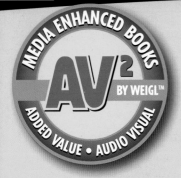

Log on to www.av2books.com

AV² by Weigl brings you media enhanced books that support active learning. Go to www.av2books.com, and enter the special code found on page 2 of this book. You will gain access to enriched and enhanced content that supplements and complements this book. Content includes video, audio, weblinks, quizzes, a slide show, and activities.

AV² Online Navigation

Audio
Listen to sections of the book read aloud.

Book Pages
AV² pages directly correspond to pages in the book.

Video
Watch informative video clips.

Key Words
Study vocabulary, and complete a matching word activity.

Embedded Weblinks
Gain additional information for research.

Try This!
Complete activities and hands-on experiments.

Quizzes
Test your knowledge.

Slide Show
View images and captions, and prepare a presentation.

AV² was built to bridge the gap between print and digital. We encourage you to tell us what you like and what you want to see in the future.

Sign up to be an AV² Ambassador at www.av2books.com/ambassador.